Irritating neighbours and fond husbands, hot-blooded housewives and religious maidens, intrepid cavalrymen and Rosa the cow — all are commemorated in *Last Laughs*, a rambling collection of epitaphs from four continents and four centuries. Bill Tidy's original cartoons add a hilarious dimension to the sentiment, wit, absurdity or plain ill-humour of our forefathers' final remarks to their passing fellow men and women.

Last Laughs

RUSSELL ASH

ILLUSTRATED BY
BILL TIDY

London
UNWIN PAPERBACKS
Boston   Sydney

First published in Great Britain as *Dead Funny* by Ash & Grant,
1974
First published by Unwin Paperbacks, 1984
Reprinted 1984

UNWIN ® PAPERBACKS

40 Museum Street, London WC1A 1LU, UK

Unwin Paperbacks
Park Lane, Hemel Hempstead, Herts HP2 4TE, UK

George Allen & Unwin Australia Pty Ltd
8 Napier Street, North Sydney, NSW 2060, Australia

© Text: Russell Ash and Ian Grant, 1974

© Illustrations: Bill Tidy, 1974

British Library Cataloguing in Publication Data
   [Dead funny]. Last Laughs.
1. Epitaphs   2. English wit and humor
I. Last laughs   II. Ash, Russell
III. Tidy, Bill
929.5   PN6291

ISBN 0-04-827123-3

Set in 11 on 13 point Goudy Old Style by A. J. Latham Ltd,
Dunstable
and printed in Great Britain by
Cox and Wyman Ltd, Reading

INTRODUCTION

Thomas Sherrer Ross Boase, formerly President of Magdalen College, Oxford, who died a few years ago, was famed for his charming and slightly inane smile, and for his genius in coining truisms. When Sir John Betjeman said that the new Waynflete Building of Magdalen was a hideous eyesore that would ruin Oxford for ever, Boase replied mildly,

'Oh, I don't know, John, it's not as ugly as it looks, you know.'

An Indian undergraduate was reported to him for being idle and incompetent. He commented,

'You really shouldn't be *both*, Mr Banerji.'

So when Boase began his book *Death in the Middle Ages* with the sentence 'Death was a grim business in the Middle Ages', there was much sniggering in common rooms over what was taken to be an award-winning new Boasism. Who, wits asked each other, was likely to welcome with screeches of joy the onset of bubonic plague? But as usual there was an edge to the banality. With the long historical perspective which he was able to take, Boase knew that, although we are still suffering the hangover of Victorian mawkishness about death, and therefore take a view almost as gloomy as the medieval, one doesn't have to go far back in history to find an age when death was a riot of fun; when the person must have gurgled with ill-suppressed mirth as he tossed the proud and angry dust into the pit, while the mourners were shaking with irrepressible guffaws (as in Bill Tidy's cover cartoon) at the pungent epitaph the local carver had hacked on the stone. The recent film about 'Punch' Miller, the jazz trumpeter, showed how jolly a thing a funeral can still be in a not too sophisticated community. The fearfulness of death can be compensated or at least disguised by a little black levity.

'Who cared about the corpse? The funeral made the attraction', wrote Byron in *The Vision of Judgment*.

Writers linger on for a little while in what they have written; others, only in what is written about them; and it's just bad luck if your tombstone happens to be in a Yorkshire churchyard exposed to ferocious wuthering. It is also very hazardous to have a name like Spark or Pease. Humbert Wolfe wrote,

> Not Helen's wonder
> nor Paris stirs,
> but the bright untender
> hexameters.
> And thus, all passion
> is nothing made,
> but a star to flash in
> an Iliad.

All very well, but at least Paris and Helen had Homer to write them up; what if your lot is a jobbing epitaphist who decides that your whole life, loves, dreads and achievements can be encapsulated in one silly rhyming joke? The religious themselves are not above playing this trick. In an old cemetery at Bilbao is an epitaph which reads,

> Aqui Fra Diego reposa
> Jamás hizo otra cosa.

(Here rests Friar James. He never did anything else.)

In many of the epitaphs, while the chisel ceased chipping centuries ago, one can still hear the axe grinding. There is religious propaganda of the 'Reader take heed' type; the reader is 'put in minde of humane frailtie' as William Camden said (quoted by John Weever in his *Ancient Funerall Monuments* of

1631). There are paeans of hate to the departed, as in the itemized denunciation by William Bond of his unprepossessing sister-in-law, quoted in full in this book. Severe practical warnings are given—against inadequate fencing around wells, wrong prescriptions, thin ice, and 'burglarizing', which could still draw down summary justice from a trigger-happy squireen. 'Inconsolable' widows advertised on tombstones that business would continue as usual—though not, perhaps, precisely the business suggested in Bill Tidy's cartoon (p.55).

In the late 18th and early 19th centuries, epitaph-hunting became a popular sport of the leisured classes. Examples were published in the *London Chronicle* and the *Gentleman's Magazine*, which makes such a telling appearance in the epitaph of Viscountess Downe (p.85). Some of the clergy strongly resented this practice, rather as some today dislike brass-rubbing. The Rev. Legh Richmond wrote in *Annals of the Poor* (1814):

> I have often lamented, when indulging a contemplation among the graves, that some of the inscriptions were coarse and ridiculous; others, absurdly flattering . . . What can be more disgusting than the too common spectacle of trifling, licentious travellers, wandering about the churchyards of the different places through which they pass, in search of rude, ungrammatical, ill-spelt and absurd verses among the gravestones; and this for the gratification of their unholy scorn and ridicule!

Church-crawlers today are not just looking for laughs, but also for fragments of social history and good amateur verse. I recently went on an epitaph hunt in the west of England. Dorset is Thomas Hardy country, and the church of Bere Regis contains the tombs of the Turbervilles, perhaps kinsmen of that Bryan Turberville of St James's, Westminster, celebrated in the epitaph on p.14. In the church of Queen Camel, Somerset, is a splended epitaph to Humphry Mildmay, lord of the manor:

> He sustain'd severall Wounds in the Warrs for his Loyalty to his Prince King Charles the first particularly at Newbury Fight, where he served as Major under his Uncle ye Earle of Cleveland, and was taken up among the slain. d.1690 aged 67 . . .

A more humble stone, in the graveyard of St Clement's in Moresk, Cornwall, commemorates Elizabeth Gay, a servant:

> Here lye the Remains of Elizabeth Gay who after a service of forty years finding her strength diminished with unparalleled distinterestedness requested that her Wages might be proportionately lessened. d. July 7 1790. As a testimony of their Gratitude for the Care she took of them for their tender years, this Stone is Erected by the Surviving Daughters of her late Master and Mistress Christopher and Elizabeth Warwick of Park in this Parish.

In the churchyard of St Andrew's, Ashburton, Devon, are two stones commemorating John Winsor, Sergemaker (d.1772) and Miriam Adams 'who for Forty four Years discharged the responsible duties of letter-Carrier to the Post Office in this town with uniform cheerfulness and strict fidelity (d.1838 aged 77).' Truro Cathedral contains a monument to Edwy Arthur West, 'formerly a chorister of this cathedral church who in the wreck of the S.S Titanic passed through the Great Waters. April 15, 1912.'

Such modern public scolds as Malcolm Muggeridge are fond of telling us that 'Death has replaced sex as the new pornography.' In other words, while everyone chatters freely about sex, death has become a taboo subject—an exact reversal of the Victorian situation, in which an obsessive interest was taken in the minutiae of death and funeral obsequies—every last detail, as it were—but talk of sex was confined to dirty jokes with the port, or to those covert volumes from whose republication the Drs Kronhausen and their publishers have lately made many an honest penny. This book goes far to disprove the scolds. We are talking about death again, even laughing at it. If death is the new pornography, funny epitaphs are its dirty jokes.

BEVIS HILLIER

My husband
promised me
that my
body should
be cremated
but other
influences
prevailed

(Emily Spear, d. 1901, aged 64)

Glendale Cemetery, Cardington, Ohio

DONALD ROBERTSON
Born 11th January, 1785. Died 4th June, 1848
aged 63 years

He was a peaceable quiet man and to all appearances a sincere Christian. His death was very much regretted, which was caused by the stupidity of Laurence Tulloch of Clotherton, who sold him nitre instead of Epsom salts, by which he was killed in the space of 3 hours after taking a dose of it.

Cross Kirk burial ground, Esha Ness, Shetland

Lord, she is Thin.

(Susannah Ensign, d. 1825)

Presbyterian churchyard, Cooperstown, New York

In memory of
JULIUS LEE
who was exploded
in a powder
mill
July 13, 1821
AE 21

Old Cemetery, Southwick, Massachusetts

In memory of **THOMAS THEOBALD**, merchant, eldest son of Peter Theobald of Lambeth, who married Martha, daughter of Thomas Turner of Lincoln's Inn Esq., by whom he had issue 7 sons and 2 daughters, who after six voyages to India and ten years residence there, returned 20 Jul. 1727 and amidst ye gratulations of his friends, resigned to death ye 9 Sep following.

St Mary the Virgin, Lambeth, London

Sacred
to the Memory of
THOMAS SHELDON
(late of Sheffield)
who died
while on a Journey
at the Golden Lion Inn,
in this Town,
Febry the 5th 1828
Aged 53 years
"In the midst of life we are in death"
This Stone was erected
by a few commercial friends, as
a tribute of respect.

St Matthew's, Ipswich, Suffolk

Devoted Christian mother who whipped
Sherman's bummers with scalding water while
trying to take her dinner pot which contained a
hambone being cooked for her soldier boys.

(Rebecca Jones, d. 1890, aged 78)

Pleasant Grove Cemetery, Raleigh, North Carolina

BRYAN TURBERVILLE, late of St. James Westminster Gent. deceased, did by his last will and testament bearing date of 20 Oct. 1711 give and bequeath to this parish of Lambeth £100 for ever to be laid out in purchase and the interest thereto for the putting out yearly two poor boys apprentices. His children also have given £100 more for the better putting out the said boys as aforesaid. Provided Rector and churchwardens shall mention this and keep the setting of this place fairly carved in a legible hand setting forth this bequest in default of which the said legacy is to become the right of St Margaret Westminster. N.B. None to be to the chimney-sweepers, watermen or fishermen and no Roman Catholic to enjoy any benefit thereof. A.D. 1719.

St Mary the Virgin, Lambeth, London

This stone is designed
by its durability
to perpetuate the memory
and by its colour
to signify the moral character
of
MISS ABIGAIL DUDLEY
who died Jan 4, 1812
aged 73

Old Hill Burying Ground, Concord, Massachusetts

Sacred to the memory of **HESTER FISHER** of Waterhouse, also of **ANNE ROTHERY** wife of N.P. Rothery, R.N. and of **ELIZABETH ANN ROTHERY** their daughter, who were unfortunately drowned at Chepstow on the evening of Saturday Septr. 20th 1812 after hearing a sermon from Philippians 1st chapter 21st verse.

Monkton Combe, Somerset

Sacred
To the Memory of
MARIA
Widow of Baker John Littlehales Esqre.,
And daughter and sole heiress
Of Bendall Martyn Esqre.
She was a lady of rare endowments,
Both of body and mind,
But eminently distinguished
For her piety, meekness and charity.

(d. Nov 11, 1796)

St Michael's, Highgate, London

This town was settled in 1748 by Germans who
emigrated to this place with the promise and
expectation of finding a prosperous city, instead
of which they found nothing but wilderness.

(Rev. John Starman, d. 1854, aged 72)

Old German Cemetery, Waldorboro, Maine

Here lyeth the bodie of **JOHN MIDDLETON**
the childe, borne 1578 dyede 1623. Nine feet
three.

Hale churchyard, Lancashire

Below lyes for sartin
Honest old Harting,
And snug close beside un,
His fat wife, a wide one.
If another you lack,
Look down and see Jack;
And further a yard,
Lyes Charles who drank hard.
And near t'un lies Moggy,
Who never got groggy,
Like Charles and her father,
Too abstemious the rather,
And therefore popp'd off
In a tissickey cough.
Look round now and spy out
The whole family out.

Ditchling, Sussex

Anything for a change.

New Gray Cemetery, Knoxville, Tennessee

The deceased being asked on the evening of his arrival in Waverly where he was going answered here and no farther.

When your razor is dull
  and you want to shave
Think of the man
  that lays in this grave.

For there was a time
  It might have been whet
You was afeared of a dime
  And now it's too late.

(August Hefner, d. 1856, aged 70)

Evergreen Cemetery, Waverly, Ohio

In Memory of **MR NATH. PARKS**, aged 19,
who on 21st March 1794 being out a hunting and
concealed in a ditch was casually shot by
Mr Luther Frink.

Elmwood Cemetery, Holyoke, Massachusetts

In Memory of **WILLIAM FRENCH**
Son of Mr Nathaniel French; Who Was Shot at
Westminster, March ye 13th 1775, by the hands
of Cruel Ministereal Tools of Georg ye 3d; in the
Corthouse, at a 11 a Clock at Night, in the 22d
year of his Age.

Here William French his body lies.
For murder his blood for vengeance cries.
King Georg the Third his Tory crew
Tha with a bawl his head shot threw.
For liberty and his country's good
He lost his life his dearest blood.

Westminster, Vermont

Here lies **ESTHER**, the wife of James Roberts
Forty-six years. She was a loving wife, a tender
Mother, a good Housekeeper — and Stayed at
Home.

Ollerton, Nottinghamshire

She was very Excellent for Reading and
Soberness

(Mary Brooks, d. 1736, aged 11)

Hill Burying Ground, Concord, Massachusetts

ASAD EXPERIENCE WILSON
1895   1946

(Given this name because he was illegitimate)

Idlewild Cemetery, Hood River, Oregon

Here lies **JOSEPH,** Anthony Myonet's son;
Abigail his sister to him is come.
Elemental fire this virgin killed,
As she sat on a cock in Stanway's field.

Winchcombe, Gloucestershire

JONATHAN RICHARDSON, 1872, aged 82,
Who never sacrificed his reason at the altar of
superstition's God, who never believed that
Jonah swallowed the whale.

East Thompson, Connecticut

To the memory of **WILLIAM BACON** of the
Salt Office, London, Gent., who was killed by
thunder and lightning at his window 12 Jul. 1787
aged 34 years.

St Mary the Virgin, Lambeth, London

SOLOMON TOWSLEE JR. who was killed in Pownal Vt. July 15, 1846, while repairing to grind a scythe on a stone attached to the gearing in the Woollen Factory. He was entangled. His death was sudden and awful.

Pownal, Vermont

Sacred to the memory of **MRS SARAH WALL**, the old and faithful but ill-requited servant of Lord Carrington who departed this life June 1832 aged 70 years.

Langley Marish, Buckinghamshire

Here lies **JOHN HIGGS**,
A famous man for killing pigs,
For killing pigs was his delight
Both morning, afternoon and night.
Both heats and cold he did endure,
Which no physician could ere cure.
His knife is laid, his work is done;
I hope to Heaven his soul has gone.

(John Higgs, pig-killer, d. 26 November, 1825, aged 55 years)

St Mary's, Cheltenham, Gloucestershire

The wedding day decided was,
The wedding wine provided;
But ere the day did come along
He drunk it up and died did.
    Ah Sidney!   Ah Sidney!

(Sidney Snyder, d. 1823, aged 20)

Providence, Rhode Island

The Unfortunate Miranda
Daughter of John and Ruth Bridgeman Whose
  Remains
are here interred, fell a prey to the flames that
consumed her Father's Hoose on ye 11th of June
1791, aged 28.

The room below flamed like a stove
Anxious for those who slept above
She ventured on ye trembling floor
It fell, she sank and rose no more.

Vernon, Vermont

He rests in pieces.

(Allegedly an epitaph to a man blown up with
gunpowder)

Exact location unknown

LIZZIE ANGELL   **JOHN ANGELL**
d. 1932   In God's Workshop
I don't know how to die.

East Derry, New Hampshire

HENRY HARRIS d. 1837 aet. 15
Killed
by the kick of a colt
in his bowels

Peaceable and quiet, a friend to his father
and mother, and respected by all who knew
him, and went to the world where horses don't
kick, where sorrows and weeping is no more.

Ross Park Cemetery, Williamsport, Pennsylvania

Sacred to the memory of inestimable worth of
unrivalled excellence and virtue, **N. R.,** whose
ethereal parts became seraphic May 25th 1767.

Litchfield, Connecticut

In Mem. of **JOSEPH,** son of Joseph and Mary
Meek, who was accidentally drowned in the
cistern of the day school adjoining this church,
April 30th 1845, aged 8 years. This distressing
event is recorded by the minister, as an expression
of sympathy with the parents and caution to the
children of the school—a reproof to the
proprietors of the open wells, pits and landslips;
the want of fencing about which is the frequent
cause of similar disaster in these districts; and as a
memento to all of the uncertainty of life, and the
consequent necessity of immediate and
continued preparation for death.

Bilton, Warwickshire

Here lies the body of **MARY ANN
LOWDER**
Who burst while drinking a Seidlitz powder.
Called from this world to her heavenly rest.
She should have waited till it effervesced.

Burlington, New Jersey

RUTH S. KIBBE
wife of
Alvin J. Stanton
May 5, 1861
Apr 5, 1904
The Lord don't make any mistakes

South Plymouth, New York

Office up stairs

(Dr Fred Roberts, d. 1931, aged 56)

Pine Log Cemetery, Brookland, Arkansas

CAROLINE H.

Wife of Calvin Cutter, M.D.
Murdered by the Baptist Min-
istry and Baptist Churches as fol-
lows:— Sept. 28, 1838. Aet. 33.
She was accused of Lying in
Church Meeting, by the Rev. D.D.
Pratt and Deac. Albert Adams—was
condemned by the church un-
heard. She was reduced to pov-
erty by Deac. William Wallace.
When an expert council was
asked of the Milford Baptist
Church, by the advice of their com-
mittee, George Raymond, Calvin
Averill and Andrew Hutchinson,
they voted not to receive any com-
munication upon the subject:
The Rev. Mark Carpenter said
he thought as the good old Deac.
Pearson said "we have got Cutter
down and it is best to keep him
down". The intentional and
malicious destruction of her
character and happiness, as above
described, destroyed her life.
Her last words upon the subject were "tell the truth & the
iniquity will come out".

Elm St Cemetery, Milford, New Hampshire.

RICHARD KENDRICK was buried August 29th, 1785 by the desire of his wife, Margaret Kendrick.

Wroxham, Norfolk

Dear Friends and companions all
Pray warning take by me;
Don't venture on the ice too far
As 'twas the death of me.

(John Rose, d. 27 January 1810, aged 10)

Reigate, Surrey

This is what I expected but
not so soon

(William Reese, d. 1872, aged 21)

Westernville, New York

Going, going, GONE!

(Epitaph to an auctioneer)

Greenwood, Hampshire

Underneath this pile of stones
Lie the remains of Mary Jones;
Her name was Lloyd, it was not Jones
But Jones was put to rhyme with stones.

Launceston, Tasmania

DOROTHY CECIL. Unmarried as yet.

Wimbledon, London

CAPT THOMAS STETSON
who was killed by the fall of a tree
d. 1820 a. 68
Nearly 30 years he was master
of a vessel & left that
employment at the age
of 48 for the less hazardous
one of cultivating his farm.
Reader remember man
is never secure from the
arrest of death.

Old Cemetery, Harvard, Massachusetts

He left his hose, his Hannah, and his love
To sing Hosannahs in the world above.

(Epitaph to a hosier)

St Michael's, Aberystwyth, Cardiganshire

Here lays **JOHN TYRWITT,**
  A learned divine;
He died in a fit,
  Through drinking port wine.
Died 3rd April, 1828, aged 59 years.

Malta

God is Omnipotent, Omniscient, Omnipresent
Electric Fluid in his life principle man which
ceased to act through the organization of
Dr George W. Gale of Exeter, N.H. Aug. 5
1873 aged 80 years, son of Capt. Jacob Gale
of East Kingston, N.H.
The breath of life is the breath of life. After it
ceased to act in the formation of dust, which
returned to earth from which it was taken. Man
has no power independent of any other power.

Exeter, New Hampshire

In life a jovial sot was he
He died from inebriete
A cup of burnt canary sack
To earth from Heaven would bring him back

(John Webb, an inkeeper)

Cheshire

ELIZABETH,
the wife of Richard Barkland,
passed to eternity on Sunday, 21st May, 1797,
in the 71st year of her age.
Richard Barkland,
the ante-spouse uxorious,
was interred here 27th January, 1806,
in his 84th year.
William Barkland
brother to the preceding, Sept. 5th 1779,
aged 68 years.

When terrestrial all, in chaos shall exhibit
    effervescence
Then celestial virtues, in their most refulgent
    brilliant essence
Shall with beaming beautious radiance thro' the
    ebullition shine;
Transcending to glorious regions beatifical sublime;
Human power absorbed defficient to delineate
    such effulgent lasting spirits;
Where honest plebians ever will have precedence
    over
Ambiguous great monarchs.

(Richard & Elizabeth Barkland, 1779)

Ercall Magna, Shropshire

For the other fellow
(*Aaron J. Beattie Sr., d. 1950, aged 50*)
Elm Lawn Cemetery, Bay City, Michigan

Know posterity, that on the 8th of April, in the
year of grace 1757, the rambling remains of the
above John Dale were in the 86th yeare of his
pilgrimage, laid upon his two wives.

Bakewell, Derbyshire

Here lies I
JONATHAN FRYE
Killed by a sky
Rocket in my eye-socket.

Frodsham, Cheshire

Sudden and unexpected was the end
Of our esteemed and beloved friend.
He gave to all his friends a sudden shock
By one day falling into Sunderland Dock.

Whitby, Yorkshire

Though shot and shell around flew fast
On Balaclava's plain,
Unscathed he passed to fall at last,
Run over by a train.

Martham, Norfolk

This gallant young man gave his life in the attempt to save a perishing lady.

Bodmin, Cornwall

Killed by means of a Rockett.

(Simon Gilkes, d. 5 November, 1696)

Milton Regis, Kent

Papa – did you wind your watch?

(Charles B. Gunn, d. 1935, aged 88)

Evergreen Cemetery, Colorado Springs, California

ELIJAH BARDWELL d. 1780

Having but a few days survived ye fatal night, when he was flung from his horse; and drawn by ye stirrups, 26 rods along ye path, as appeared by the place where his hat was found and here he had spent ye whole of the following severe cold night treading down the snow in a small circle. The family he left was an aged father, a wife and three small children.

Montague, Massachusetts

ROSA
My first Jersey Cow
Record 2lbs 15oz Butter
From 18qts 1 day milk

Central Village, Connecticut

Here lies the body of **ALEXANDER MACPHERSON**
He was a very extraordinary person.
He was two yards high in his stocking-feet,
And kept his accoutrements clean and neat.
He was slew
At the battle of Waterloo:
He was shot by a bullet
Plumb through his gullet:
It went in at his throat
And came out at the back of his coat.

Exact location unknown, Scotland

ASENATH
widow of
Simeon Soule
Died
Feb 25, 1865
Aged
89 years 11 mo.
& 19 days.
The Chisel can't help
her any.

Mayflower Cemetery, Duxbury, Massachusetts

Let this small monument record the name
Of Cadman, and to future times proclaim
How, by an attempt to fly from this high spire,
Across the Sabrine stream, he did acquire
His fatal end. 'Twas not for want of skill,
Or courage to perform the task, he fell;
No, no! A faulty cord drawn too tight
Hurried his soul on high to take her flight
Which bid the body here beneath, good night.

(Epitaph to a tightropewalker, killed 1739)

St Mary Friars, Shrewsbury, Shropshire

ANNE HARRISON well known by the name
of Nanna Ran Dan, who was chaste but no prude;
and tho' free yet no harlot. By principle virtuous,
by education a Protestant; her freedom made her
liable to censure, while her extensive charities
made her esteemed. Her tongue she was unable to
control, but the rest of her members she kept in
subjection. After a life of 80 years thus spent, she
died 1745.

Easingwold, Yorkshire

Here lies buried in the tomb,
A constant sufferer from salt rheum,
Which finally in truth did pass
To spotted erysipelas.
A husband brave, a father true,
Here he lies; and so must you.

Baton Rouge, Louisiana

In memory of **CHARLES H. SALMON,** who was born September 10th, 1858. He grew, waxed strong, and developed into a noble son and loving brother. He came to his death on the 12th of October, 1884, by the hand of a careless drug clerk and two excited doctors, at 12 o'clock at night in Kansas City.

Morristown, New Jersey

Of such is the kingdom of Heaven
Here lie the remains of **THOMAS CHAMBERS**
Dancing Master
Whose genteel address and assiduity in teaching
Recommended him to all that had the
Pleasure of his acquaintance.
He died June 13, 1765, Aged 31.

Llanbedlig, Carnarvonshire

The mortal remains of
JOHN BRINDLE;
After an evil life of 64 years
Died June 18th, 1822,
And lies at rest beneath
This stone.

St Giles' Cemetery, King's Road, London

They lived and they laugh'd while they were able.
And at last was obliged to knock under the table.

Newbury, Berkshire

Here lies the body of **MARY ELLIS** daughter of
Thomas Ellis & Lydia, his wife, of this parish. She
was a virgin of virtuous character & most
promising hopes. She died on the 3rd of June
1609 aged one hundred and nineteen.

Leigh, Essex

This tomb was erected by William Picket, of the
City of London, goldsmith, on the melancholy
death of his daughter, Elizabeth. A testimony of
respect from greatly afflicted parents.

In memory of **ELIZABETH PICKET,** spinster,
who died December 11, 1781. Aged 23 years.
This much lamented young person expired in
consequence of her clothes taking fire the
preceding evening. Reader — if ever you should
witness such an affecting scene; recollect that the
only method to extinguish the flame is to stifle it
by an immediate covering.

Stoke Newington, London

She was a lady of Spiritual and cultivated mind, and her death was instantaneous, arising from fright occasioned by a violent attack made upon her house door by three or four men in a state of intoxication with a view to disturb the peaceful inmates in the dead of night.

Long Buckby, Northamptonshire

ASA WHITCOMB, a Pillow of the Settlement

Barnard, Vermont

In memory of **MR. NEH. HOBART,** who
   died Jan. 5, 1789
in the 72 yr. of his age
whose death was caused by falling backwards,
   on a
Stick, as he was loading wood. Nobody present
   but his
grandson, who lived with him.
A kind husband, a tender parent, a
trusty friend, respectable in his
day, his death remarcable!

Pepperell Center, Harvard, Massachusetts

In memory of   who died of cholera
   morbus caused by eating green fruit. In the
certain hope of a blessed immortality. Reader, go
   thou and do likewise.

Grantham, Lincolnshire

How shocking to the human mind
The log did him to powder grind.
God did command his soul away
His summings we must all obey.

(Elisha Woodruff, d. 1816, aged 70)

Old Burial Ground, Pittsford, Vermont

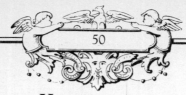

Here lie the bodies
of **THOMAS BOND** and **MARY** his wife.
She was temperate, chaste and charitable
But
She was proud, peevish and passionate.
She was an affectionate wife and tender mother
But
her husband and child, whom she loved,
Seldom saw her countenance without a
disgusting frown,
Whilst she received visitors, whom she despised,
With an endearing smile.
Her behaviour was discreet towards strangers;
But
Independent in her family.
Abroad, her conduct was influenced by good
breeding;
But
At home, by ill temper.
She was a professed enemy to flattery,
and was seldom known to praise or commend;
But
The talents in which she principally excelled
Were differences of opinion, and discovering
flaws and imperfections.
She was an admirable economist,
And, without prodigality,
Dispensed plenty to every person in her family
But
Would sacrifice their eyes to a farthing candle.

She sometimes made her husband happy
With her good qualities;
But
Much more frequently miserable — with
her many failings
Insomuch that in 30 years cohabitation he
often lamented
That maugre all her virtues,
He had not, in the whole, enjoyed two years
of matrimonial comfort.
At length
Finding that she had lost the affections of her
husband,
As well as the regard of her neighbours,
Family disputes having been divulged by
servants,
She died of vexation, July 20, 1768,
Aged 48 years.
Her worn-out husband survived her
four months and two days
And departed this life, November 28, 1768
in the 54th year of his age.
William Bond, brother to the deceased, erected
this stone, as a *weekly monitor* to the
Surviving wives of this parish,
That they may avoid the infamy
Of having their memories handed to posterity
With a Patch-work Character.

Horsley-Down Church, Cumberland

Some called him Garrett, but that was too high,
His name was Jarrett that here doth lie:
Who in his life was tost on many a wave,
And now he lies anchored here in his own grave.
The Church he did frequent while he had breath
He desired to lie therein after his death.
To heaven he is gone, the way before
Where of Grocers there is many more.

St Saviour's, Southwark, London

Let her R.I.P.

Exact location unknown

Trumpets shall sound,
And archangels cry,
"Come forth, Isabel Mitchell,
And meet William Mattheson in the sky".

West Churchyard, Tranent, East Lothian

My good lads, do not sit upon this stone on
account you do disfigure it with your heels; lean
on it if you please.
Yours, &c
R. Pocock.

North Curry, Somerset

Sacred to the memory of
MR JOHN STEVENSON, late of this parish,
who was unfortunately killed by a stag at
Astley's Amphitheatre, 6 Dec. 1814
aged 49 years.

St Mary the Virgin, Lambeth, London

Here lies one wh
os life thrads
cut asunder she
was stroke dead
by a clap of thunder

(Mary Hale, d. 1719, aged 38)

Green Cemetery, Glastonbury, Connecticut

In memory of J
Aged 787 years

Malmesbury Abbey, Wiltshire

Stop here, ye Gay
& ponder what ye doeth
Blue lightnings flew &
Swiftly seized my Breath
A more tremendous
flash will fill the skies
When I and all that sleep in death shall rise

(Simon Willard, d. 1766, aged 60)

Bow Wow Cemetery, Sheffield, Massachusetts

His inconsolable widow dedicated this
monument to his memory and continues the
same business at the old stand,
167 rue Mouffetard.

(*Pierre Cabochard*)

Père la Chaise, Paris

RICHARD BASSET, the old sexton of this parish, who had continued in the office of clerk and sexton for the space of forty-three years, whose melody was warbled forth as if he had been thumped between the shoulders with a pair of bellows, was buried on 20th September, 1866.

Sussex

In memory of **MARY ANN,** a Native Woman aged 38 years, built by John Macleod.

Dum-Dum burial ground, West Bengal, India

Here lies the man Richard,
And Mary his wife;
Their surname was Pritchard,
They lived without strife;
And the reason was plain, —
They abounded in riches,
They had no care or pain,
And his wife *wore the breeches*.

Chelmsford, Essex

THOMAS WOOD. Formerly a bather at this place.

St John's Church, Margate, Kent

Here lies the body of **JOHN MOUND**
Lost at sea and never found.

Winslow, Maine

JOSEPH PALMER. Died Oct. 30, 1873, aged
84 yrs. and 5 mos. Persecuted for wearing the
beard.

Leominster, Massachusetts

Sacred to the memory of **ANDREW CRAIG,**
late spirit merchant in Edinburgh, who, by
persevering industry and strict integrity in all his
dealings, raised himself to a respectable station in
society. In the relative duties of domestic life,
kindness of heart was his distinguishing
characteristic. He was an affectionate husband, a
tender parent, a kind master and a faithful friend;
while his frank, unreserved, and affable manner,
combined with fascinating social qualities,
endeared him to all his acquaintances.
Died 24th March, 1830, aged 45 years.

Greyfriars churchyard, Edinburgh

Sacred to the Memory of
MISS
ELIZABETH TUCKER
Who died
July 29, 1834
aged 47 years
Like a good steward what the Lord gave her
she left in the bosom of the church.
$1200.

Massachusetts

Here lies the body of **RICHARD HIND,**
Who was neither ingenious, sober or kind.

Cheshunt, Hertfordshire

Here lie the bones of one, poor Louch,
A cricketer so staunch,
That vexed his hands should miss the ball,
He caught it in his paunch.

*(Louch was killed by a blow in the stomach from a
cricket ball, in the 1880s)*

Rochester, Kent

Died of Grief
Caused by a Neighbour
Now Rests in Peace

(Louisa Adler, d. 1933, aged 60)

Palm Springs, California

Here lies the body of **THOMAS VERNON,**
The only surviving son of Admiral Vernon.

(d. 23 July, 1753)

Plymouth, Devonshire

JULIA ADAMS. Died of thin shoes,
April 17th, 1839, aged 19 years.

New Jersey

This Blooming Youth in Health Most Fair
To His Uncle's Mill-pond did repaire
Undressed himself and so plunged in
But never did come out again.

(Abial Perkins, d. 1826, aged 13)

Center Cemetery, Plainsfield, Vermont

In memory of **MR
JOSEPH GRAPP** – ship
wright who died ye 26th of
Novbr 1770 Aged 43 years

Alas Frend Joseph
His End was Allmost Sudden
As though the mandate came
Express from heaven
his foot it slip, And he did fall
help help he cried & that was all.

Mylor Creek churchyard, Cornwall

Save me O God, the mighty waters role
With near Approaches, even to my soul:
Far from dry ground, mistaken in my course
I stick in mire, brought hither by my horse.
Thus vain I cry'd to God, who only saves:
In death's cold pit I lay ore whelm'd with waves.

(1730)

Wick St Lawrence Church, Somerset

Here lies **RUFUS SWEET** and **WIFE**
They fed the hungry and
clothed the naked
and fought secret societies
And here may they rest until
Gabriel blows his horn

(Rufus Sweet, d. 1884)

Hope Cemetery, Perry, New York

In memory of the old fish:
Under the soil the old fish do lie
20 year he lived and then did die
He was so tame you understand
He would come and eat out of your hand.
Died April the 20th 1855.

Blockley, Gloucestershire

Those that knew him best deplored him most

(John Young, d. 1836)

St Andrew's churchyard, Staten Island, New York

Under this stone lieth the Broken
Remains of **STEPHEN JONES** who had
his leg cut off without the Consent of
Wife or Friends on the 23rd October
1842 in which day he died. Aged 31 years.
Leader I bid you farewell. May
the Lord have mercy on you in the
day of trouble.

St John's churchyard, Chester, Cheshire

Here lies ye Precious Dust of
THOMAS BAILEY

A painfull Preacher	A most desirable neighbor
An Exemplary liver	A pleasant companion
A Tender Husband	A common good
A careful Father	A cheerful doer
A brother for Adversity	A patient Sufferer
A faithful Friend	Lived much in a little time

A good copy for all Survivors

(Thomas Bailey, d. 1688, aged 35)

Old Burying Ground, Watertown, Massachusetts

Here lies the body of **WILLIAM GORDON,**
He'd a mouth almighty and teeth accordin';
Stranger, tread lightly on this sod
For if he gapes you're gone, by God.

Reading, Berkshire

His illness laid not in one spot,
But through his frame it spread,
The fatal disease was in his heart,
And water in his head.

Whitby, Yorkshire

Here lyes the Body of **LEWIS GALDY ESQR.**
who departed this life at Port Royal the 22nd
December 1739. Aged 80. He was born at
Montpelier in France but left that Country for his
Religion and came to settle in this Island where
He was swallowed in the Great Earthquake in the
Year 1692 and by the Providence of God was by
another shock thrown into the Sea and
Miraculously saved by swimming until a Boat
took him up. He Lived many Years after in Great
Reputation. Beloved by all that knew him and
much Lamented at his Death.

St Peter's churchyard, Port Royal, Jamaica

Sacred
To the Memory of
EDWARD FITZGIBBON ESQ.,
who died the
19th of November, 1857, aged 54.
Author of numerous works on angling
and was better known as
Ephemera
This
monument
is erected by a few of his friends
in admiration of
his piscatory writings

Highgate Cemetery, London

Been Here
and Gone
Had a Good Time

(Dr J. J. Subers, d. 1916, aged 78)

Rosehill Cemetery, Macon, Georgia

Here lies **PHEBE,** wife of David Ames, who was
a succorer of many and of Brother Osgood also.
She died October 20, 1838.

Osgoodite Cemetery, Canterbury, Connecticut

In memorie of the Clerk's son
Bless my iiiiii
Here I lies
In a sad pickle
Killed by an icicle

(Unnamed, 1776)

St Michael & All Angels, Bampton, Devonshire

Buried in this churchyard, **HUGH MACKENZIE,** born 4 July 1783, died 27 Aug. 1814, shortly after he had begun to distinguish himself at the Bar of England; of excellent talents; of character pure, sincere, placid, diligent, just, benevolent, religious; blameless as far as it can be said of human nature.

Greyfriars churchyard, Edinburgh, Midlothian

Here lies the body of **ROBERT MORE,**
What signifys more words?
Who kill'd himself by eating of curds:
But if he had been rul'd by Sarah his wife,
He might have lived all the days of his life.

Dundalk, Louth, Ireland

Near this place lies **CHARLES CLAUDIUS PHILIPS,** whose absolute contempt of riches, and inimitable performances on the Violin, made him the admiration of all who knew him. He was born in Wales, made the tour of Europe, and, after the experience of both kinds of fortune, died in 1732.

Wolverhampton, Staffordshire

Capt Samuel
Jones' Leg which
was amputated
July 7 1804

Old Cemetery, Washington, New Hampshire

Against his will
Here lies **GEORGE HILL**
Who from a cliff
Fell down quite stiff;
When it happen'd is not known,
Therefore not mention'd on this stone.

St Peter's, Isle of Thanet

In memory of **ANNA HOPEWELL**:
Here lies the body of our Anna
Done to death by a banana
It wasn't the fruit that laid her low
But the skin of the thing that made her go.

Enosburg Falls, Vermont

Suddenly fell asleep in Jesus at the Pinner
Railway Station, while waiting for a train to
return to London.

Brompton Cemetery, London

Weep, stranger, for a father spilled
From a stage coach, and thereby killed;
His name was John Sykes, a maker of sassengers,
Slain with three other outside passengers.

Wimborne Minster, Dorset

In Memory of **MR PETER DANIELS**
Born August 7, 1688. Died May 20, 1746.

Beneath this stone, a lump of clay,
Lies Uncle Peter Daniels,
Who too early in the month of May
Took off his winter flannels.

Medway, Massachusetts

Gone to be an angle.

(Gertrude Walker, d. 1893)

Lt. John Walker Cemetery, White Horn, Tennessee

The private sleeping chamber of
RICHARD HISLOP, Islington.

Highgate Cemetery, London

In the garden here below
Water me that I may grow;
When all grace to me is given,
Then transplant me into heaven.

Charlton Kings, Gloucestershire

To **LEM S. FRAME,** who during his life shot 89 Indians, whom the Lord delivered into his hands, and who was looking forward to making up his hundred before the end of the year, when he fell asleep in Jesus at his house at Hawk's Ferry, March 27, 1843.

Exact location unknown (USA)

Our little Jacob has been taken from this earthly garden to bloom in a superior flower-pot above.

Maine

Here lies poor, but honest **BRYAN TUNSTALL;** he was a most expert angler, until Death, envious of his Merit, threw out his line, hook'd him, and landed him here the 21st day of April 1790.

Ripon Cathedral graveyard, Yorkshire

In Memory of **WILLIAM BINGHAM,**
Surgeon to the Fever Hospital, Pancras Road,
Who departed this life May 31st, 1821, aged 28
years
His death was occasioned by the puncturing his
finger,
While sewing up a dead body.

St Giles Cemetery, Kings Road, London

Here lies **MRS. BUFF,** who had money enough;
   She laid it up in store:
And when she died she shut her eyes
   And never spoke no more.

(She was a fortune teller)

St Mary's, Nottingham, Nottinghamshire

Died on the 11th inst., at his shop, No. 20, Greenwich Street, **MR. EDWARD JONES,** much respected by all who knew and dealt with him. As a man he was amiable; as a hatter upright and moderate. His virtues were beyond all price, and his beaver hats were only three dollars each. He has left a widow to deplore his loss, and a large stock to be sold cheap, for the benefit of his family. He was snatched to the other world in the prime of life, just as he had concluded an extensive purchase of felt, which he got so cheap that his widow can supply hats at a more reasonable rate than any house in the city. His disconsolate family will carry on business with punctuality.

Exact location unknown (USA)

In memory of
ABRAHAM RICE
who departed this life
in a sudden and Awful
manner and as we trust
enter'd a better June ye 3, Anno D, 1777
in ye 81st year of his age.

(Rice was killed by lightning)

Framingham, Massachusetts

Now Aint
That Too Bad

(Charles DuPlessis, d. 1907, aged 53)

Rosehill Cemetery, Chicago, Illinois

Neglected by his doctor,
Ill treated by his nurse,
His brother robbed the widow,
Which made it all the worse.

Dulverton, Somerset

RANSOM BEARDSLEY
Died Jan. 24 1850
Aged 56 yrs. 7 mo. 21 days
A vol. in the war of 1812
No pension

Mottville, Michigan

This disease you ne'er heard tell on –
I died of eating too much mellon.
Be careful, then, all you that feed – I
Died because I was too greedy.

Chigwell, Essex

Unknown man shot in
the Jennison & Gallup Co's store
while in the act of burglarizing
the safe Oct. 13, 1905
(Stone bought with money
found on his person)

Sheldon, Vermont

Here lies the carcase
Of Honest **CHARLES PARKHURST,**
Who ne'er could dance, sing,
But always was true to
His Sovereign Lord the King
Charles the First

(d. December 20th, 1704, aged 86)

Epsom, Surrey

JOHN BLAIR
Died of Smallpox
Cowboy Throwed Rope
over Feet and dragged him
To his Grave

Boothill Graveyard, Tombstone, Arizona

Here lyes the Body of **WILLIAM SPEKE,** aged
18, Son of Hy. Speke Esq. Captain of His
Majesty's Ship Kent; He lost his Leg and Life in
that Ship at the capture of Fort Orleans the 24th
of March Anno. 1757

St John's Church, Calcutta

Here lies the body of **SAMUEL YOUNG** who came here and died for the benefit of his health.

Ventnor, Isle of Wight

In memory ov
JOHN SMITH, gold digger, who met
weirlent death neer this spot
18 hundred and 40 too. He was shot
by his own pistill.
It was not one of the new kind
but a old fashioned
brass barrel, and of such is the
Kingdom of Heaven

*(Exact location unknown. Said to be near Sparta,
California)*

Once ruddy and plump
But now a pale lump,
Here lies **JOHNNY CRUMP**
Who wished his neighbour no evil;
What tho' by death's thump,
He is laid on his rump,
Yet up he shall jump,
When he hears the last trump,
And triumph o'er death and the devil.

Worcestershire

Through Christ, I'm not inferior
To William the Conqueror.
(*Rom.* viii. 37.)

Cupar, Fife

WILLISTON WINCHESTER
Son of Antipas and Lois Winchester. Born 1822,
Died 1902. He never married.
"Uncle Wid"
One of nature's noblemen, a quaint old-
fashioned, honest and reliable man. An ideal
companion for men and boys. Delighted in
hunting foxes and lining bees.

Marlboro, Vermont

In Memory of **MR EBENEZER TINNEY**
who died March 12, 1813, aged 81 yrs.

My virtue liv's beyond the grave
My glass is rum.

Grafton, Vermont

Her neighbors and friends stood weeping and
showing the coats and garments which she made
while she was with them.

(Rebecca Corey, d. 1810)

Middle Cemetery, Lancaster, Massachusetts

In honoured memory of
SARAH J. ROOKE
Telephone Operator
Who perished in the flood waters
of the Dry Cimmaron at Folsom
New Mexico, August 27, 1908
while at the switchboard warning
others of the danger. With heroic
devotion she glorified her calling
by sacrificing her own life that
others might live.

Folsom, New Mexico

A real unpretending and almost unconscious good sense and a firm desire to act right on all occasions to the best of her judgement were her most distinguished characteristics, hereditary personal grace of both form and face which even in age had not disappeared completes her picture. For her character and other particulars see the Gentleman's Magazine for May, 1812.

(Viscountess Downe, d. 1812)

York Minster, York

Hail!
This stone marks the spot
Where a notorious sot
Doth lie;
Whether at rest or not
It matters not
To you or I.
Oft to the "Lion" he went to fill his horn,
Now to the "Grave" he's gone to get it warm.

Beered by public subscription by his hale and
stout
companions, who deeply lament his absence.

Tonbridge, Kent

PROF. JOSEPH W. HOLDEN,
Born Otisfield Me. Aug. 24, 1816,
Died Mar. 30, 1900.

Prof. Holden the old Astronomer
discovered that the Earth is flat
and stationary, and that the sun
and moon do move.

Elmwood Cemetery, East Otisfield, Maine

WARREN GIBBS
died by arsenic poisoning
Mar. 23, 1860
Ae. 36 yrs. 5 mos. 23 d'ys.

Think, my friends, when this you see
How my wife hath dealt by me
She in some oysters did prepare
Some poison for my lot and share
Then of the same I did partake
And Nature yielded to its fate
Before she my wife became
Mary Felton was her name.
Erected by his brother, Wm. Gibbs

Pelham, Massachusetts

JOSHUA
Son of Mr Joshua
& Mrs Anna Miller
who was killed with a
Sawmill May 26th
AD 1781 in the 15th
year of his age

Old Farm Hill Cemetery, Middletown, Connecticut

To the Memory
Of the late **MR JOHN STEVENS,**
Celebrated corn operator,
And many years resident
Of this parish, who departed
This life February 21st, 1813
Aged 81 years

St Andrew's Cemetery, Grays Inn Road, London

Here lies a man of good repute
Who wore a No. 16 boot.
'Tis not recorded how he died,
But sure it is, that open wide,
The gates of heaven must have been
To let such monstrous feet within.

Keeseville, New York

AARON S. BURBANK
1818   1883

Bury me not when I am dead
Lay me not down in a dusty bed
I could not bear the life down there
With earth worms creeping through my hair

Winsted, Connecticut

Sacred
to the memory of
EDWARD HUNT
late of Islington
who died a Martyr to the Gout
August 18th, 1848, aged 53 years.

Highgate Cemetery, London

Capt. John Cleves Symmes was a Philosopher and the originator of "Symmes' Theory of Concentric Spheres and Polar Voids". He concluded that the Earth was hollow and habitable within.

(John Cleves Symmes, d. 1829, aged 49)

Hamilton, Ohio

Here lies **DAME MARY PAGE,** relict of Sir Gregory Page, Bart. She departed this life March 4th, 1728, in the 56th year of her age. In 67 months she was tapped 66 times. Had taken away 240 gallons of water, without ever repining at her case, or ever fearing the operation.

Bunhill Fields, London

Grieve not for me father dear
Nither my mother while you'r hear
Though sudden death on me did call
Which happened by a falling wall
Weep not therefore it is in vain
Weep for your sins and them refrain.

(1720)

Clapton-in-Gordano, Somerset

A sacred truth! now learn our awful fate!
Dear Friends, we were first cousins, and what not —
To toil as masons was our humble lot;
As just returning from a house of call,
The parson bade us set about his wall;
Flushed with good liquor cheerfully we strove
To place big stones below and big above;
We made too quick work — down the fabric came,
It crush'd our vitals — people bawled out, shame!
But we heard nothing — mute as fish we lay
And shall lie sprawling till the judgement-day.
From our misfortune this good moral know,
Never to work too fast or drink too slow.

*(Thomas & Richard Fry, d. August 25th, 1776, aged
19 & 21)*

Nr Bath, Somerset

Here lies in a state of perfect oblivion John Adams who died Spt. 2 1811 aged 79. Death has decomposed him and at the great resurrection Christ will recompose him.

Newbury, Massachusetts

ROTHWELL
WILLIAM P. ROTHWELL M.D.
1866-1939
This is on me.

R.

Oak Grove Cemetery, Pawtucket, Rhode Island

Here lie the remains of honest **JOE MILLER,** who was a tender husband, a sincere friend, a facetious companion, and an excellent comedian. He departed this life the 15th day of August, 1738, aged 54 years.

(On the comedian, Joseph Miller)

King's College Hospital, London

Gone home.

Grafton, Vermont

P. S.
The Old Nuisance

(Philip Sydney Bennett; erected at his own direction, to perpetuate the insulting description of him by his son-in-law, who reportedly asked his wife how long the old nuisance would be around).

East Calais, Vermont